The Blessings of a Single Parent

*A book of inspiration written from one
who has been there*

by
Maxine Bethea

Aspect Books
Ringgold, GA

Copyright © 2010 Aspect Books
ISBN-13: 978-1-57258-497-6
Library of Congress Control Number: 2010915108

Published by
Aspect Books

Contents

Dedication

This book is dedicated to all my children and family members for their support and encouragement during the process of writing this book. Truly, your love is the real blessing of this single parent, and I praise God for each of you. I love you.

This book was written in the memory of my parents, Tommie and Mable Lewis, who really taught me the true meaning of parenthood. It was their consistent spiritual efforts that trained me and kept me striving when I felt I couldn't go on with the struggle. Now, thanks to them, I'm praising God for the hard times and for showing me that God can take my many messes, make it into a message, and allow me to be HIS messenger. That, too, was another blessing for this single parent.

Acknowledgements

I'd like to give many, many thanks to those who motivated and encouraged me to put my life's experiences in the form of a book. There have been three people who felt that my story could inspire other single parents, and God confirmed that idea in so many ways:

Dr. Conrad Gill
Southern Union Conference
Director of Education
Atlanta, Georgia

Dr. Samuel Darby
Great Valley Middle School
Guidance Counselor
Malvern, Pennsylvania

Dr. Marie Redwine
Southwestern Adventist University
Adult Degree Program, Former Director
Keene, Texas

Special thanks also to my typists Cassandra Morris and my daughter Purette D. Mills. Thanks, is not a big enough word for the editing job done by Purette as well! I love you, both!

Introduction

In the following pages you will find every physical, mental, social, and spiritual need that one can experience on this earth. The amazing fact about each of those needs is that through trials and tribulations, God—in His time—was meeting everyone. Those blessings were literally miracles in my life.

My personal story (**her**story, not **his**tory) is one that I feel will help single parents to have more faith in Jesus than in themselves and it will encourage readers to let Jesus lead them through their many trials.

There will be many similarities in the lives of the single parent. The difference comes in to play in how we handle each event. Be aware of the fact that this book really is not about Maxine Bethea as much as it is about the God who loves Maxine Bethea. The great news is that He loves you, too, and what He's done for others, He will do for you.

Be faithful. Be encouraged. Be blessed!

Chapter 1

Family Background

I was born in Gainesville, Florida, on March 25, 1934. I had one brother and a sister who were born ahead of me, Tommy C. and Leola, both now deceased. There were two boys before them who passed. I did not know them. Their names were J. B. and Moses. My parents, Tommy and Mable Lewis, were two remarkable people. Daddy was a construction worker who helped build most of the bridges in Georgia. Mom was a talented housewife and an outstanding musician who raised twelve children, eight girls and four boys. She was the organist, pianist, and choir director along with many other responsibilities for our local church. In my mind there was nothing she could not handle.

My oldest brother, Tommy, was our second father when dad traveled to Georgia for work the entire week and returned home on the weekends. My sisters' names are Leola, Vernell, Martha, Annette, Joyce, Mable, and Carol; my brothers are Tommy, Joseph, Henry, and Lemuel.

We lived in a very small four-room house. There were two bedrooms, one for Mom and Dad and one for the twelve of us. Dad made a small petition to separate the girls from the boys in our little room.

I can remember a certain eventful occasion every year at about the same time when Mother would cry out in pain. My oldest sister, Leola, and I would get in trouble for peeping through the crack in the wall. Mom was in labor with a child. I often wondered why Mom kept having babies if it was so painful. Of course, I found out when I got married and started a family of my own. Wow!

I have always been thankful for my large family but more than that I was thankful for my praying parents. Even though as a child I did not understand why Daddy prayed so long, as I grew older I began to appreciate those prayers, especially when I became a mother and wife.

Both my grandparents and parents were God-fearing people. My paternal grandmother, Lottie Lewis, actually began a church for our family in her living room on S.E. 3rd Avenue in Gainesville, Florida. God blessed us along with a few other members to build the Bethel Seventh-day Adventist Church. Along with my grandmother, my maternal grandfather, Charles Manns, was among the founders of this church.

It was because of the small church community and the closeness of its members that I can truly parallel that same warmth and intimacy to what could be found in the Lewis' household. Just as we made sure that our church members were cared for at all times, twice as much concern was given to the needs of each family member. I praise God for the little lighthouses that often represent the true family relationship.

When I was but a youth during the Depression, I recall times at home being very difficult for us. In those days families could receive "stamp books" to make purchases for necessities. Each family member had one. Yes, we got fourteen books (thank God for a large family). We were given nine books just for shoes, clothes, bread, sugar, flour, meal, etc. With Dad working hard for about $150 a week digging ditches, laying bricks, and making cement for bridge building, and Mom teaching us how to stretch a dollar, we were able to survive and at times even thrive because we were such a happy and loving family.

My paternal grandmother, Lottie Lewis, lived next door. She was always inviting the visiting preachers to her house for Sabbath dinner after church services. Every thing had to be just right when the preacher and his family came to dinner. Any preacher who came to the South Atlantic Conference territory in the 1920s and 1930s was Grandma Lottie's special guest, and we had to be on our best behavior. Papa Charles Manns and Grandma Louise Manns were a blessing to us as well. They would take time to teach us to love, respect, and be obedient to Christ. As we walked from the east side of town to the west side of town for weekly church services, we also learned at a young age the importance of time. We could not be late because Grandma Louise would have started playing the piano for Sabbath School and my siblings and I were the song service leaders. Tardiness was not accepted.

Thanks to our Lord and Savior for God-fearing parents and grandparents who consistently disciplined us and taught us respect for worship, time, and all people. This is the heritage that set the foundation for who I am today.

To have had both maternal and paternal grandparents that knew Jesus, gave me the direction I needed in my life to stay close to God, family, and the Christian church. This is why Bible work, prison ministry, and many other community service activities have become my life's passions. Caring for others is now synonymous with my name because of the spiritual seeds planted by my family. These are the blessings that shaped me as a single parent.

Chapter 2

Educational Background

My first school was Duval Public Elementary School. We had one large room for grades 1–6 with one teacher, Mrs. Duval. We prepared our own breakfasts (grits and powdered eggs) and lunches at the school. That was an experience

Duval Public Elementary School

that I will never forget. When the enrollment at Duval reached more than capacity, I was transferred to another school, Williams Elementary. This was a blessing for me because Dad was building a new four-bedroom house for our family, and it was within walking distance of my new school.

What excitement! I was blessed to be in a new house and a new school. There was real joy in my heart. Williams Elementary School had more of a family spirit; that is, everyone knew each other and we were already somewhat bonded.

The May Pole

In school I was very active, especially in sports. No one wanted to hit a ball outfield. It didn't matter whether the hit landed to the left, right, or center field. They knew if the ball came my way or anywhere near me, I would catch it. I loved sports, and I also loved the tradition we called "Planting the May Pole." Everyone enjoyed the beauty of this activity. It consisted of students taking one of many colorful ribbons and moving in a pattern around a tall pole around, over, and under their schoolmates to make a lovely design. It was so much fun and so exciting.

We had a wonderful and patient teacher named Mrs. McClendon. Our principal was Mr. Cook, a man who took no foolishness. He very seldom smiled. You did not want the teacher to send you to the office to see Mr. Cook. He did not tolerate disrespect from anyone. If you came late you better have a good written excuse, and he knew every parent's signature.

Daddy was still building our home, and we would pass the site on the way to school. I remember every lunch hour I was excused to run home and take Daddy his lunch in the hot, hot sun, but I did not mind, because Daddy was building our new house. By the time I began high school that grand day had finally come and we moved in our new home on 1331 SE 3rdAvenue. This house was built with my dad's own hands, and what a joy to see my mother so happy.

There was a lot of love and praying in our new house, so much so that my mother decided to share some of that love with her five nieces and one nephew when their mother died by allowing them to live with us as immediate family members. Now there were eighteen of us—this was when we really had to share everything: our clothes, food, beds, books, and toys. This was really tough for me. I was just beginning high school and once again my room was overcrowded. Well, it taught me to be thankful, how to share with others, and not to be selfish. It was during this time that I had to really help my parents.

While continuing my education in high school, I found myself even more active than I was in the elementary. After school I had to practice as a band member, cheerleader, basketball player, majorette, and drill team member. I also had to make time to work somewhere. The Lord blessed me to find a job fixing dinner for a very nice couple. They paid me $18.50 a week. I gave my mother $16.00 and kept $2.50. From this I would paid my tithe and offering and kept $.50 for myself.

One of my fondest memories during my secondary education was of my relationship with my best friend, Mamie Thower. The two of us loved to dress alike for school. We would go downtown and buy a couple of yards of material and make gathered skirts with our hands, iron press them and off we would go to school looking like twins.

My years at Lincoln High were very rewarding and filled with physical excitement. Mamie and my other classmates nicknamed me "Rabbit" because of my basketball skills, which included running and jumping very high. I probably looked like a rabbit while my #13 jersey was in fast motion. My classmates would shout, "Go, Rabbit" when our team took over the court.

Being a part of that kind of enthusiastic school spirit was extraordinary, but after the game my fun would come to an abrupt halt. You see, everyone went to Wabash Hall to celebrate and socialize, but I had always been instructed to come straight home when the game ended due to the lateness of the hour. When Mom saw how upsetting that was to me, she eventually made a deal with me. As long as I was home by midnight, I was able to stay and socialize with my friends. This was the greatest deal ever. Of course this did not go unnoticed by my siblings, who now also wanted the same privilege, but they realized soon enough that they, too, would have to become an athlete first.

Finally, my biggest moment in life came at that time. Graduation day was here. I had arrived. Wow! It was on that day that I wore my very first pair of stockings. I also found myself with two really skinny legs (not to mention other body parts that seemed undeveloped).

Lincoln High School

After graduation mom and dad wanted me to join my sister Leola at Oakwood College all the way in Huntsville, Alabama, but there was no money for that kind of education. There were now twenty people in my parent's household to  care for and feed. I knew that I had to get a job somewhere. My friends thought that getting a job was the wrong thing to  do, but I knew that it was the best thing for me to do at that time for my family.

Chapter 3

New York City: My New Life

My Aunt Lena, who lived in New York, visited us often. On one of her visits she asked me if I would like to go back to New York, and she would help me find a job there. That was an answer to my prayer. So soon after gradation I took off for the "Big Apple." What a bad experience that was for me. The first few months after coming from the south where people are very friendly to an overcrowded city where people pass you by and don't even say good morning was one of my first awakening moments; this was an insult. My Aunt Lena told me to stop saying good morning, hello, and how are you today? She said that no one would respond. Mentally, I was already postured to return home.

As time passed the Lord blessed me to find my first job through my sister-in-law Georgia Mae, who really helped me. I began working in a clothing factory on Canal Street. While working I met the man of my dreams, Lunue Fentress Bethea. I called him Lenny. He blew my mind when he talked to me in

11

French. My fancy expression told him that I didn't understand a word he said, and then he told me in English that he would like to date me. He was a butcher who worked very hard. We dated for a while, then he popped that most important question that every woman wants to hear, "Would you marry me?" I told him that the two of us would have to talk to my mother and father, and he agreed.

I called my parents in Gainesville, and they spoke to him. They then gave me the ok to go ahead and get married. We got married on July 25, 1953, at 520 W142nd Street. What a beautiful day that was for me. Our marriage was perfect. God blessed our union with four beautiful daughters: Purette, Debra, Vera Lunue, and Belinda.

As our family grew, my husband and I decided to move out of the city to Brooklyn because there were more trees and grass for growing children to play. The new home, located at 170 Sumpter Street, was very nice. Life for me in New York was now great. I came to this big city and found a job, a husband, and the blessings that children bring. Praise God from whom all blessings flow.

The children were pleased with their new home and community and even though my husband traveled by subway to Manhattan, New York, to work each day, he enjoyed returning to our family's new location, too.

We attended church each week and were active in all of its programs and activities. The entire family and extended

New York Camporee
Maxine Bethea (left)
and Cecila Slone (right)

family members were all involved in the Pathfinder Club. My sisters, brother, and I were directors and deputy directors. There were five Master Guides in our family. This is the highest level one could reach in this organization. What fun and joy we had training God's children how to survive in the "time of trouble"! Glory to God for the spiritual memories made at the Mount of Olives Seventh-day Adventist Church in Brooklyn, New York.

Induction Day at Capitol City Church (left to right):
Brenda Simpson, Pathfinder Leader;
Elder Conrad Gill, Lake Region Conference
Youth Director; Maxine Bethea, Inductee

My induction as a Master Guide

Chapter 4

Shaken, But Blessed

At the age of two, my daughter, Vera Lunue, became ill, and the Lord allowed her to go to sleep in Him. This was extremely difficult for me as a young mother. The pain was unbearable, but God's comfort was a blessing and helped me regain my footing day by day. However, after having four girls and many months later, my wonderful Savior blessed me again with the gift of a son. What an answer to prayer! The nurses at the Brooklyn King's County nicknamed him "Cochise" because of his beautiful Indian red complexion and curly black hair. We legally named him Fentress Lunue Bethea III.

As our family grew, we moved into our own beautiful little home, and we enrolled our children into the local school that was directly across the street from my new job at the neighborhood candy store. It became known as Max's candy store (which was named after me, Maxine). What a time I had with the students before, after, and during the school day. They would pile into that little candy store, and everyone would demand service at the same time. I loved it and felt that this was a heaven-sent job created just for me. Here was another one of His tailor-made blessings.

It was during those years when I experienced many changes that shook my world. I was forced to make some very difficult and big decisions. My marriage was beginning to fall apart. My husband became an alcoholic and was very abusive toward me. Our finances were now more and more unsure as money was being spent to support the alcohol and later a gambling addiction as well. We decided to separate as these violent ordeals were beginning to affect not only my emotional and physical health but the needs and the health of our children as well. This now meant that I had to work a second job in order to take care of our basic family needs.

This search for a second job began my journey that would prepare me to receive His future blessings for me as I moved in the direction of becoming a single parent. I did not know that then but can plainly see in retrospect that what I was about to face was going to take me through a series of wonderful yet painful experiences that eventually placed me in position to become a topnotch salesperson and provider. How did this happen, you say? Let me explain.

This job was a part-time position as a salesperson for the Century Metalcraft Corporation. My supervisors, Director Leon Bishop and his assistant, Mrs. Jesse Fleming, were wonderful people. This job placed many of its workers in competition with one another to be the best salespeople of Presto Pride cookware, and Jesse and I were always close in our numbers of sales. Our competition motivated us (as well as the other workers) to be the best and led us to become the closest of friends. For three years, month after month, my name would appear as the #1 salesperson of the company. Needless to say, this eventually allowed me to put my life back together again. God's blessings were now falling all around me.

Salesperson for presto pride-selling this product brought in the extra money needed to care for my children. What a blessing!

It was during this progressive time of my life that Satan tried to discourage me once again with a triple attack. The first involved my new best friend, Jesse. While she was on her way to bring items to very needy families of the local church, she was involved in a tragic and fatal head-on collision and was killed instantly upon impact. There was no way I could continue to work under such horrid and painful memories of Jesse at that corporation again. So, I began again to search for another opportunity to become financially independent for what now seemed to be an inevitable separation from my husband. After those three years he was still spiraling downward and away from us as a family. My focus more now than ever was on saving and protecting the lives of my children.

My husband was willing to be hospitalized in order to get the help he needed to recover from his addictions. He was truly a wonderful father and husband without those dependent habits. Unfortunately, before his full recovery took place, he died in 1965 and left me to raise four children alone: Purette (11 years), Debra (9 years), Belinda (7 years), and Cochise (5 years). I had some serious questions for Jesus at this grievous time in my life. It was hard for us to raise the children together, how in the world could I do it alone at the tender age of 30 years?

God answered every question. Listen single parents. When you pray, God does hear, and He does answer your prayers. Believe me. He led me to His Word: Isaiah 54:4-6. He told me not to fear anymore because my Master would be my husband. From that day to this very day of your reading this page, I have learned to trust in the name of Jesus Christ. He has and will always be there for me. There is no "busy signal" when I call upon Him, and I can make that call at any time. This is a blessing for all people, but it was a special one for me during this dark period of my life.

Chapter 5

Educating My
Children God's Way

I can clearly remember one day after receiving counsel from my pastor concerning my family plans, he strongly encouraged me to consider placing my four children in church school. He stated the facts about Christian education that convinced me that this would be their protection from the painful world in which they now had to face with the absence of their father. To affirm this necessity, my oldest daughter came home from public school one day and boldly stated that she did not want to attend public school anymore because of the influences of alcohol, drugs, and smoking in and around the school. This confirmed what I already knew.

With little money as income and my daughter making such a demand, what was a single mother to do? I knew I had to do something and do it quickly, so after much prayer, God directed me to Brooklyn Temple Seventh-day Adventist School. I

Brooklyn Temple Elementary School
My children's first Christian Seventh-day
Adventist institution.

went to the school with only a prayer in my heart and no money in my purse.

Knowing the large expenses that I would incur in church school, I nervously explained my situation to the principal and told him that I would be willing to do anything to put my four children in church school; the Lord touched his heart. He told me that he could use some help in his office and also could use me as a teacher's aid, and I jumped at the chance. In exchange for a full-time salary, I was compensated with full tuition for all of my children. Once again, God rained down from heaven this wonderful blessing for me, a single parent.

However, the enemy (Satan) was still trying to discourage me, because no salary meant no income for food, transportation, clothing, or any other important necessities for basic living. After much prayer concerning this dilemma, my next answer came from God when the principal needed someone to prepare lunch for the students and approached me about the job. Once again, this new task was for no cash payment but a free daily lunch for the entire family. I thanked God for such a quick answer to prayer and decided to continue to let go of the rest of my concerns and give all of my needs to Jesus.

That day when I got home a lady called and informed me that my name was referred to her by the school principal as someone who may be able to transport her children to and from the school for a fee. Soon after our arrangement, other parents needed similar services. It was not long before I began transporting five families in a 1968 Ford station wagon, and it was that blessing that enabled me to pay for the transportation and gas while assuring my own children means to get to school every day. Praise the Lord!

As my car began to show signs of deterioration, Mrs. Louise Boyer, a parent of a son that I was transporting, found herself with a 1972 brand new Buick

My gift from God (another blessing) because I obeyed HIS command and put my children in church school even though I could not afford it.

Electra 225 that she was now unable to drive due to a physical condition that she had recently incurred, and she insisted that I have it not only for the purposes of school transporting but to keep as my own family vehicle as well. All good and perfect gifts come from above. That was only God using her to answer, bless, and encourage my faith once more while now making an income (from helping others) of $350 per week. All I could say then, and all I can say now is THANK YOU, JESUS!

It was shortly after this incident that Mrs. Boyer took ill, and it was getting more and more difficult for her to care for her 5–year-old son. She approached me to ask if Kevin could stay with me in order for him to have consistent care, schooling, and parenting. I wanted to help so I took Kevin in my home as my own son. When his mom died, I continued educating him in Christian schools as she wanted. He lived with me until he was 18 years old.

Little did I know how the experiences I had at Brooklyn Temple Elementary School were preparing me for becoming

Northeastern Academy, New York City, New York

a teacher, a better parent, and an administrator. You see, as Brooklyn Temple increased its enrollment, it became overcrowded, and we found it necessary to expand and start a new school; so, the principal, Mr. Silvera, and three other teachers

(Annette Wilson, Oneida Lewis, and myself) left Brooklyn Temple to open its sister institution, Gold Street Seventh-day Adventist Elementary School—now a part of Hanson Place Academy. It was here that I received the on-the-job training I needed to continue to provide for my family.

By this time my two oldest children had made it to high school and were able to attend Northeastern Academy, and they graduated from that grand institution. Because of the two- to two-and-a-half-hour commute to this same school, I did not enroll my third child at Northeastern Academy. Instead, I sent her to school in Miami, Florida, where she lived with my sister Vernell and her fam-

ily. This city was the home of another fine Christian school, Greater Miami Academy. However, when I moved to Indianapolis, Indiana, in 1973, I discovered Cicero Academy, another Seventh-day Adventist (boarding) school that offered the quality education that I had come to demand for each of them, and I decided to enroll Belinda, her brother, Cochise, and my nephew, Robert (better known as "Speedy") who lived with us at that time.

When I left all three of them on campus that day, a burden was lifted as I drove home. This incredible institution was able to work out a payment plan for me that enabled all three students to fully register and live in the dorm. This plan included each child working on campus to aid in this enormous expense. Eventually all three graduated from Cicero Academy and moved on to attend Oakwood College. It pays to obey God! Praise HIM!

Indiana Academy-Cicero, Indiana
(Boarding School)

Almost coinciding with this time period, I was trying to enroll my oldest daughter at Oakwood College (now called Oakwood University). This is the same Christian institution that all of our family members proudly attended. We left home with $200 and a letter stating my financial arrangements. Upon arriving on campus, I walked into the president's office (who was none other than Calvin Rock) and explained my plight, which included my small pittance. He told me that I needed a minimum of $1,000 to enroll her for that first semester. Again, I explained that I only had $200 and a financial arrangement letter that I then gave to him. Then, I started to pray. I told Pastor Rock that God told me

24

to bring her to Oakwood College in my car, and if she had to go back to Brooklyn, he would have to take her. "Just please give her a chance at success," I said. He smiled and said to me that either I was crazy or I had a strong faith in God! He then excused himself to talk with the "brethren."

About 30 minutes later he came back into the office and told me they decided to give her that chance for one semester. Now that was a direct answer to prayer from my Lord and Savior. Before leaving the president's office, I asked if we could have prayer, and I gave God the praise for using Pastor Rock. Then I fully registered my daughter and took her to her new room while crying and giving praise to His name with every step. Then, after a final prayer with my child, I kissed her goodbye, got into my car, and drove back to Brooklyn alone with no earthly partner, but with plenty of angels and God's company, while singing His praises all the way home. That was another blessing for this single parent!

Blake Center
Oakwood College Campus
(2009-Oakwood University)

25

My daughters (left to right):
Purette (oldest), Debra (middle), Belinda (youngest)

My one and only son, Fentress Lunue Bethea.

Purette
*Principal, Guidance
Counselor, Teacher,
Children's Ministries'
Coordinator
Huntsville, AL*

Debra
*Correctional Officer,
Cosmetologist
Indianapolis, IN*

Belinda
*Women's Ministry
Coordinator/Evangelist,
Motivational Speaker,
Dialysis Clinical Specialist
Gainesville, FL*

Fentress (Cochise) the III
*City Manager of Mililani,
Hawaii*

27

My children, granddaughter, Skynetta, and me.

Chapter 6

Blessings of Ministry

In 1969 God began to stretch me in many directions. I had no previous plans to work with prisoners, study to become a Bible worker, or direct summer camp programs, but God  was doing a "new thing" in my life. He was not only taking care of the monetary needs for the family, He knew that I wanted to develop a better relationship with Him and thus provide for the spiritual needs of my family as well.

Camp Experiences

God directed me to be a major part of two regional conference junior camp programs: Camp Victory Lake in the Northeastern Conference and Camp Wagner in the Lake Region Conference. Elder Owen Troy, Pastor Timpson, Pastor Gouldbourne, Pastor Peay, Pastor Gilbert, and Ruby Foster were responsible for giving me my first opportunities to lead youth at Camp Victory Lake. And under the leadership of Camp Directors Conrad and Mildred Gill and Lane Todd, working at the Lake Region Junior Camp at Camp Wagner in Cassopolis, Michigan, was a real and rewarding learning experience as well. The positive social, physical, and spiritual memories created at both of these Christian camps trained and prepared me for bigger and more responsible jobs that were yet to come.

The best times at each camp were the Camp Council sessions, annual banquets, early morning line calls, and the sunrise and sunset flag raising and lowering ceremonies. Backwards Day, Christmas in July, hayrides, midnight surprise pajama parties, 6 a.m. morning hikes, skating parties, and oh boy, the good old-fashion socials were thoroughly enjoyed by the campers and the staff. Every activity was planned to the very last detail so that every age group could have maximum clean, pure, and healthy fun!

One exciting experience at Camp Wagner was when our activity director, my daughter Purette, and Camp Director Conrad Gill planned a candy bar extravaganza! That is, they rented an airplane and directed the pilot to fly it over the campground's open field. This is where every camper and counselor stood in their respective lines waiting for a surprise from the sky. As the plane dipped low, the campers could see oversized candy bars falling from the sky, and once the plane cleared three huge drops, the campers were released to race across the field and gather all they could carry! It was a memory created like no other, and not just a memory for the campers but for every adult present as well.

Junior camp was so very exciting! Our campers may have cried a little when they were dropped off by their parents, but when camp was over, no one wanted to leave and calls were being made to see if parents would afford or could afford just one more week. All of our cabins were filled to capacity. These memorable events will be with them for the rest of their lives. Hopefully, all that was learned along with the socialization skills they received will shape them as they help and care for others in their future.

Canoeing was just one of many daily classes we had at our Seventh-day Adventist regional camps. We also had ceramics, swimming, rocketry, gymnastics, photography, and arts and crafts.

God placed me, a single mother, at these two camps to train His children and give me wonderful positive spiritual and social experiences in the process. I was receiving His blessings as He was using me to bless others! Praise God! Praise God! Praise God!

Words could never express my thanks to the many directors, counselors, and parents who trusted me with their lovely young people. I thank God for keeping us safe and unharmed on those campgrounds.

Lake Region Conference's Camp Wagner

(left to right)
Lane Todd, boys' director;
Maxine Bethea, girls' director;
Conrad Gill, camp director

Camp Hike

Camp Council

Arts and Crafts Class

Northeastern Conference's Victory Lake Camp

Camp directors, counselors, staff, and their families

Sabbath morning Prayer Circles in front of the Victory Lake Camp
Bland House before attending services.

Prison Ministry Experiences

I was recruited as a trainee under the leadership of Roy Adams to become a prison ministry counselor. It was because of this initial introduction to this ministry that I have been a prison ministry coordinator and trainer for more than forty-eight years. My children have experienced and known about the many inmates who have been baptized into God's remnant church and participated in these activities as well. They got to see firsthand how the Holy Spirit could change the lives of inmates from "crime to Christ."

It was the consistent love and encouragement of the Mount of Olives Seventh-day Adventist Church and the tremendous pastors who directed and taught pure and true ministering that allowed me to be wholly used by God. Pastors Everett Alexander, Edgar Lockett, James Edgecombe, Alvin Goldbourne, Robert Lister, Gilbert Foster, and Pastor and Mrs. Claude Thomas were all instrumental in building the spiritual natures of my family. Because of positive memories and exciting times under their tutelage, the precedence for prison ministry had been set in my heart. So I continued to minister when I relocated to Indianapolis, Indiana, where I moved to be closer to my brother, Pastor J.P. Lewis, and his family. It would be his strong male influence that would help me develop and raise my son and nephews into the men that God would have them become.

Jesus Behind Bars Program

The prison ministry work was very new in the Indiana territory, so the training classes began in order to help the men and women behind bars find the true answers to freedom. The initial meetings were held in my home and at the Eastside Seventh-day Adventist Church, and as other churches (Capitol City Seventh-day Adventist and Haughville Seventh-day Adventist) joined in the effort, the organization began to rapidly grow over a period of ten years. It was during this time that God even used one of my Sabbath hospital visits to help expand our prison ministry workforce in a very unexpected series of events. God blessed my children and me by placing us in the direct path of a beautiful elderly patient named Adeline Morris.

She was sitting on her bed smiling and waving to us as we entered her room. We found out that she had double pneumonia and no family or friends to take care of her. Jokingly, I stated to her, "Come and go home with us!" She immediately took my words seriously, and needless to say, when her doctor released her, she was placed in care. She lived with us as our newly adopted family member. From that day she lived with us for ten years, and we were her family until her life ended. Sister Adeline Morris became one of the strongest prison ministry counselors in the Lake Region Conference territory.

Prison ministry training class—(left to right) Brother Curry, Adeline Morris, and Sister Hutcherson—in my Indianapolis, Indiana, home.

In consequent years this pattern of training and growth took place when I moved to Richmond, Virginia, and later to Gainesville, Florida. It was under the leadership of Hazan Zariff that the Richmond Prison Ministry team grew to a vital soul-winning organization. Brother Jefferson, Beatrice Hunt, and many others joined us as a powerful prison ministry team in the Allegheny East Conference. We were able to counsel, give Bible studies, and baptize prisoners in several facilities: the Powhatan Correctional Facility, the James River Correctional Center, and other jails in the area. God blessed our efforts and many souls came to know Christ as a result.

If you want to be used by God in a mighty way, sign up with a prison ministry group in your local church. If you don't have one in your church, start one. To see men turn their lives around from crime to Christ is a joy I can't explain. I will forever work in the prison ministry program for the simple reason that it makes me a stronger and more determined Christian on a daily basis. Also, I have found that helping people in prison and out of prison has encouraged and strengthened my determination to continue in the way of the Lord and more anxiously await His soon coming.

Powhatan Correctional Facility

What I didn't know was that God was using me (as I was influencing my own children for ministry) in ways that I did not realize at the time, and He was just beginning to direct my path toward more and greater ministries.

It was during my first return trip to my hometown of Gainesville, Florida (as you will read in chapter 11) that this ministry continued to develop me spiritually and bring blessings to my life as a parent of teenagers and now young adults. Under the direction of Lyndon Edwards Sr., a prison ministry team of volunteers from the Bethel Seventh-day Adventist Church stretched the guidelines of this work to include a baptism plan for inmates who were ready to publicly acknowledge their total acceptance of the total truth, God's Holy Word.

We actually were able to get permission from the Gainesville prison warden to transport prisoners (with a $25 fee attached to pay for a guard and bus driver) and bring them to the Bethel Seventh-day Adventist church worship services for

James River Correctional Center

baptism and promptly return them when the service ended. What a great impact this had on the congregation, their families, the prison staff, and the other inmates. This act in itself helped to motivate this prison ministry organization to continue to grow and go forward. In the first year we had many baptisms and doubled the interest in our weekly Bible studies. Praise God!

Roy Adams trained and coordinated Seventh-day Adventist volunteers for prison ministry in the 1960s in New York City in the Northeastern Conference.

Indianapolis, Indiana, Prison Ministry Team
Lake Region Conference
(Left to right) Alberta Ellis, Francis Hughes, Sister Cook,
Director Maxine Bethea, Edward Thomas
(Not pictured: Pastor J.P. Lewis and Eugene Hughes)

Bible Worker

The second "new thing" that the Lord introduced to me (simultaneously with my prison ministry work over a period of twenty plus years) was Bible work. Early in my life I was always helping people. I have found that as I've gotten older that has not change. People are truly my business. So, when I was asked by Pastor Robert Lister back in the early 1970s to assist as a Bible worker in his revivals for the very first time, things in my life finally started to change. Working in "tent efforts" did something for my soul. As I witnessed and taught others, I was happy. I had found my true gift in serving others.

Single mothers, I want you to find your gift as well and then let God have that gift as you use it for Him to the best of your ability. If it is teaching, working in children's ministries, playing an instrument, or singing, we must remember that this is not for the praise of others or self, but to glorify God. The Lord has blessed me to be a soul-winner for His kingdom—that is, one who teaches the gospel to others. Of this I am sure. You must find your soul's calling and you, too, will be sure of God's leading. You see, this type of faith builds that special relationship with God and is reflected in the lives of our children.

If you really want to share your faith, you could also do all you can to help our youth and our senior citizens. Without these two groups of individuals in our lives, we as a people cannot go anywhere. It has been because of our senior citizens that we have the churches that we worship in today, and it will be because of our youth (rightly trained) that we will have a place in which to worship in the future.

When God called me to use my gift as a Bible worker and assist in revivals, I had to move with quick obedience. You, too, must do the same. I did not know that this ministry would take me all around the U.S. and the world field. Some of those movements were to many cities in and out of this country:

- New York City, New York (Pastor Robert Lister)
- Indianapolis, Indiana (Pastors Joseph P. Lewis, Randy Stafford, and Elder Edward Thomas)
- Seattle, Washington (Pastors Hobdy, Emile Peeler, and Wagner)
- Gainesville, St. Augustine, Bartow, Palatka, Lake City, Live Oak, and Tampa, Florida (Pastors Powell, Wells, Brisé, Vincent, E. Hall, and Mrs. Nicole Brisé)
- Richmond, Virginia (Dr. Gene Donaldson)
- Washington, D.C. (Emile Peeler)
- Baltimore, Maryland (Pastors Fred Russell and Emile Peeler)
- Jacksonville, Florida (Walter and Sandy Pearson)
- Chicago, Illinois (Walter and Sandy Pearson)
- St. Thomas, Virgin Islands (Walter and Sandy Pearson)

Bible Work Ministry on the Island of St. Thomas with Evangelists Walter and Sandy Pearson

• Ivory Coast, West Africa (Southeastern Conference Women's Ministries' Leaders Nicole Brise and Belinda Smith).

I have seen the working of the Holy Spirit change people's lives and reunite families. This encouraged me each time to do more and more for Jesus, and this is what helped to strengthen me spiritually as a young single mother. What a blessing it was and still is to serve God's people and help to hasten His soon return at the same time. Now it's your time to be blessed by ministry. You can find that ministry by giving God all your challenges. Then watch your mess become a message in someone else's life as God explodes in yours.

Baptisms in St. Thomas, Virgin Islands

Maxine Bethea, St. Thomas, Virgin Islands

Many baptisimal candidates

*Bible Work Ministry in Lynchburg and
Martinsville, Virginia, with Evangelists
Joseph and Julia Lewis*

*Sister Bethea holding the Bible
study certificates*

*Graduated class of
Bible students*

*Pastor Lewis congratulating
Bible students*

Chapter 7

Power of Fasting and Prayer

All of my children received a Christian education. Traveling to Indianapolis, Indiana, to my brother and sister-in-law Pastor J.P Lewis', home was one of the best decisions I have ever made in my life.

At the home of these two Christian people, I learned what real fasting and prayer was about. After my husband's death, I *thought* I was praying and fasting. My time at pastor and sister Lewis' home along with their church family helped me to be more dependent on my God and to develop more faith in Jesus Christ.

The church at that time had about 50 members who loved the Lord. They lived it, preached it, and shared it. They were in the process of trying to build a sanctuary for the Master. This little company of members bought land that the conference said they couldn't afford.

I never saw such a group of loving, caring, and dedicated people in my life. Even though there will always be tares in the church, one could never surmise such a thing with this congregation of saints.

As time passed and the church had their last meeting with the president concerning the new sanctuary to be built, the members mortgaged their homes, made loans, and donated their funds for this most important project.

The president was impressed but was not ready to say "go ahead." Instead, he told the church members that they had to raise $10,000 more dollars within two weeks or there would be no building.

The pastor came back to his members with a smile and told them the decision that came out of the meeting. The members were concerned, but the pastor calmly talked to them. He told them the $10,000 the president demanded would not be asked of this membership.

The pastor said he did not have a plan, but he knew that God had a plan. He asked the members to meet with him after Sabbath and he would share with them the plan God had given to him. After sunset everyone gathered together to see how they could get this amount of money in two weeks. We really don't/and sometimes still don't know what a mighty God we serve.

After a season of prayer, God spoke to His people and all He asked of them was to be obedient, to fast, and pray. The pastor asked all that could to remain until midnight.

Many stayed and they prayed, sealed and stamped envelopes for more than one hour for about 200 fundraising letters. After which we prayed again around the table of letters, loaded our cars and a slew of vehicles drove down Sherman Drive to the mailbox, and we prayed around that box and dropped in all the letters.

We were now headed for a two week fast. We then hugged and kissed each other good night and went our separate ways, each knowing we would see each other every day for the next two weeks for fasting and prayer, asking for God's will to be done.

We met Sunday evening after our first day of fasting and prayed and went home. Monday we did the same. Tuesday we started the routine, but God was at work.

I received a phone call to come home quickly. Poor me, the first thing that crossed my mind was that someone had died or some other bad news.

To my surprise Pastor Lewis had received a letter from a Catholic woman that had $10,000 enclosed and a promise of $5,000 a year until the church was paid off in full. To God be the glory!

The East Side Seventh-day Adventist Church is still standing today as a monument of what God can do when we go to Him in prayer, fasting, and obedience. Praise God.

If you really want to grow your faith, pray and fast for our youth and senior citizens. Without these two groups of people in our lives, we are going nowhere. If it were not for our seniors, we would not have the churches we worship in today. If we don't properly train our young people in the school of the prophets as Jesus has told us, we will not see our Savior's face because of disobedience.

While in Indianapolis, it was the power of fasting and prayer that led me to be employed with the IPS System as a reading and math tutor that placed me in our private school system at the Capital City Seventh-day Adventist School for ten years.

During those years much was accomplished for our students and parents. Grandparents' Day was established at that time. It was felt that grandparents were "very special" in their help and support to our school and to their grandchildren. The tutorial program was a blessing to our studentsv and to me.

This newfound power in prayer and fasting was now propelling God's work and strengthening my resolve to witness now more than ever.

Chapter 8

The Death of My Parents and My Brother

The years 1977, 1980, and 1981 were very sad for me and my family. It seemed to start in 1977 when my dad called me on the Monday before Thanksgiving and stated that he was taking my mother to my sister Vernell in Miami, Florida. He further mentioned that he was very tired and wanted to know what I thought about his plan, as if asking my permission. I agreed with Dad's decision, not knowing that he wasn't feeling well. Thanksgiving night Mom called and said, "Maxine, your dad prayed a prayer like never before . . . like it was his last prayer with us."

Mom later said to me that when Dad was headed back to Gainesville, she said, "I will not see Honey again." (She always called Daddy "Honey!") Mom was always thinking that she would "go" first; she had no idea that it would be Daddy. None of us did.

Daddy drove back to Gainesville from Miami with no problems. He and my brother Henry called me on that Thanksgiving Sunday after attending a Men's Day Service, sounding very high-spirited. I never thought that he would die on that following Tuesday from acute indigestion.

When two people live together for more than 50 years the other one left doesn't stay long afterward. My mother passed in 1980. All of the children came together and sang for both funerals. This made me remember my mother sitting at the piano with all of us gathered and singing every Friday night for worship. In 1981 my brother Tommie C. passed in New York City.

I have learned when God calls His children home, I must give thanks and honor to my Creator. He knows best. We will endure the loss by God's grace. In 1985 I moved back to Gainesville, Florida. I was back in the house that my father built with his own hands. I praise God all the time for my parents who loved us so much that they took the time to teach us about the love of Jesus.

My Parents
Mr. and Mrs. Tommie Lewis

My Brother
Mr. Tommie C. Lewis

51

Chapter 9

Coming Home

Losing so many loved ones in such a short time created a longing in me to return to my hometown of Gainesville, Florida. It was as if I was being led by God to now serve the church, city, and state that once served, educated, and trained me. This type of homecoming revived my spirit and drove me to even go back to live in the home built by my father's own hands. I knew the memories of family would surround me and bring me comfort and joy as I transitioned from the loss of family members to living without them in my life. Just the thought of planning this great return home made me feel the showers of blessings that were ahead of me.

The day finally came. In 1985 it was time to leave Indianapolis and go home.

On a nice sunny day, after hitching a rented U-Haul trailer to the back of my car, I packed up my family and my adopted senior citizen, Adeline Morris, and began the drive to my old hometown.

While driving through Nashville, Tennessee, I noticed smoke from the rear of my car. It was only Jesus who directed me off Interstate 65 South because angels awaited me there. Before I could locate a mechanic, a very friendly and concerned gentleman saw that I was having some trouble with my car. He offered to help cool the engine by putting water in my radiator. He then pointed out the location of a nearby mechanic and sent us on our way.

As I entered the mechanic's shop, a well-dressed stranger came up to me and asked me to open the hood of my car. When I did he asked my family and I to stay in the car while he went inside to talk to the owner of the shop. Within minutes he came out with a receipt in his hand in the amount of $370. He had paid in advance for my car repairs. All I could do was cry, pray, and thank him profusely. It was at that time that his friend came to check to see if everything was OK.

I was so overwhelmed with gratitude that I prayed with the men right then and there not knowing that the car repair payment was only a part of the blessing that God had in store for us. You see, the two men also took care of an overnight stay at the nearby hotel so that we could get rest while the car was being repaired. He then put the receipt in my hand and told me to use that to get my car the next morning. By this time, I was so overwhelmed with God's joy that I was over-flowing with gratefulness.

After a brief conversation with them, I found out that these two men were Baptist ministers returning to their hometown from a prison ministries' convention. What a connection! It was then that I realized that these were no ordinary men. God had literally sent two angels to rescue me. He knew I had no means whatsoever to take care of this type of an emergency, so rather than allow me to be stranded, God used the first gentlemen (who cooled the radiator) to lead me to the ministers who had the means to not only get the car restored and back on the road but to make sure we were able to rest through the night as our car was being repaired.

These men did not need gas or repairs when they stopped at that particular location. They only stopped to get something to drink. As a matter of fact, one of the men stated that this was not a place where they would usually stop. Both of us knew that God had placed them there just at that time to be a blessing to me.

Needless to say, we had found common ground in Christianity and the prison work. I insisted on getting their names and addresses so that I could repay them for such an enormous favor. One of the gentlemen made it clear that this was God's providence and His blessing to me. He further explained that any repayment would steal the joy from God's purpose in using them to share what He had given them to give me. For many years I kept in touch with those men and shared God's love with them as they continued to do the same with me. Once again, God was watching over this single parent, and I thank Him for using them to bless me in His name.

When we finally arrived in Florida, I felt the relief that can only come from God and being safe at home again. Getting resettled in such a comfortable environment was not a difficult transition at all for me. I was home.

Chapter 10

The Pine Forge
Academy Experience

After one or two weeks in Gainesville, Florida, I was blessed to get a wonderful teaching job at Heritage Christian School. After serving this institution for about one and

a half years, I received an invitation from Pine Forge A c a d e m y (PFA) in 1987 to serve as the assistant dean

of girls. Since I had just returned to my hometown and was settling into my new job and enjoying it, I did not feel impressed to relocate to Pennsylvania at that time, so I declined the offer twice. However, the persistence of the headmaster,

Elder Conrad Gill, paid off because after much prayer and supplication, it was evident to me that God wanted me at PFA.

Upon arriving onto the Pine Forge campus, my family and I were amazed at the beauty all around us and the rolling hills surrounding the great Manatawny River. There were 545 acres at that time and 265 excited young people running around the campus. What impressed me the most, however, was the awe-

The Manatawny

some mentoring of the headmaster, Conrad Gill, and his assistant, Samuel Edward Darby, for our young African-American male students. Wow, what a dream team! Now that was "a thing of beauty." To see these men meet the needs of these students with physical, mental, spiritual ideas, support, activities, routines, and a clear vision of what could be on that campus, was a rare sight on any campus, regardless of the race. This is just what Pine Forge Academy needed—strong leadership.

This administration planned skating activities, ice cream treats, weekly shopping trips, and campus industries that helped defray the tuition expenses and give students the opportunity to assist paying their own tuition. Industries such as:

- the apple orchard plan where every classification was required to spend an hour picking apples per day as a part of their daily schedule.
- J.C. Penney's—sorting and folding clothes
- Sears—sorting and folding clothes

These administrators wanted the best for each student, and it showed in all they did and tried to do, and it especially exemplified itself in the vision they had for the future of Pine Forge Academy.

I was blessed a hundred fold when I obeyed God's voice and accepted "the call" to go to this great institution. However, there were some real challenges during my five years. You see, I wore many hats while at Pine Forge Academy. I was the head dean, assistant dean, physical education assistant instructor, librarian, senior class sponsor (class of 1988), and the supervisor of many other activities. In the dorm the young ladies really tried my last bit of patience and kept me on my knees asking Jesus for the strength and endurance to go on facing each new day.

The lessons learned from my single parenting that directed my efforts and led me to eventual success with these teenage ladies. Through all the ups and downs the blessings continued to come to me in many forms, some of those being evening and morning dorm worships, counseling sessions, and even the weekly administrative Dean's Counsel meetings. Even then, God was preparing and strengthening me to be a stronger parent for more than just my children.

Parenting takes on a whole new meaning when you think of a dormitory full of young ladies between the ages of 14 and 19 years, all with many different personalities, character traits, attitudes, and internal conflicts. Mix that with being homesick, fatherless, motherless, and even parentless and you have only begun to imagine the challenges mentioned  above. So I became everything that each student needed. I was their mother when they needed someone to listen to their problems and more of a father when they needed the strong arm of discipline.

Yet, listening to them would make your heart bleed. I knew that prayer was the only answer. I prayed alone with and for the students. We often prayed in groups, groping for answers that seemed outside our reach. But prayer always gave me a great sense of hope, and I wanted that sense for the students, my daughters, as well. Just to be there working, counseling, playing, encouraging, and praying for the students was a real joy.

Young and old people are my business. Without helping someone each day of my life means that I have wasted that day and that makes my life useless. As Christians, and especially Christian parents, we must be about our Fathers' business now!

There were so many needs for our dormitory that I prayed for God to give to our ladies. Fortunately, there were also many great people who God used to answer those prayers along with a supportive administration. Air conditioners, a new boiler, educational funds for needy students, and outdoor basketball and volleyball courts were just a few of the many needed items that were supplied during my tenure. Praise God from whom all blessings flow for Leroy Owens, Elder and Mrs. Henry Fordham, Gene Smith, Reather Cheatham, Mr. and Mrs. Singleton, Mr. and Mrs. Ralph Shipman, Merwyn Arms, and Mr. Tribble. These people made major contributions to the growth and care of Kimborough Hall and created a better living experience for each young lady who dwelled there.

Then there were the "community mothers" who literally nurtured and showered the girls with love by donating treats and surprises several times per month. These ladies made sure that the girls' lives, especially during the holidays and for birthday celebrations, had a little taste of a close family life by sharing homemade goodies which made life at Pine Forge Academy very, very memorable. We even had community fathers and our male deans, Leon Thomas and Lyndon Elliott, who also parented our ladies as strong male figures and assisted the dormitory mothers in their efforts. We truly were a happy, bonded, Christian family at the beautiful Pine Forge Academy.

Dean Bethea at work in Kimborough Hall office.

Kimborough Hall, Girls' Dormitory

The beautiful Pine Forge Academy campus.

Chapter 11

It's My Turn Now

During my final year at Pine Forge Academy, I started to realize that I was in a position to do something that I had always wanted to do—complete my college education. My children were all independent working adults, and I was free, disengaged, and hungry for such an educational challenge.

It dawned on me that all of the blessings from God were preparing me for such a time as this. There were so many blessings and accomplishments in God's ministry with my family, church, and career that I felt it was my turn now to focus on personal aspirations that would allow me to return even greater ministry to the world.

By this time in my life the blessings of this single parent had taken the following path, as led by God:

- A Bible worker in New York; Richmond, Virginia; Pine Forge, Pennsylvania; Indianapolis, Terre Haute, and Muncie, Indiana; Baltimore, Maryland; Gainesville and Orlando, Florida; St. Thomas, Virgin Islands; Detroit, Michigan; Seattle, Washington; Washington, D.C.; Memphis, Tennessee; Chicago, Illinois; Ivory Coast, West Africa

- A store manager in Brooklyn, New York
- A topnotch saleswoman in Brooklyn, New York
- A teacher in Brooklyn, New York; Indianapolis, Indiana; Gainesville, Florida; and Richmond, Virginia (and the next two years in Atlanta, Georgia, and Baltimore, Maryland)
- The Dean of Women, sponsor, and an instructor at Pine Forge Academy
- A prison ministry coordinator in New York City; Richmond, Virginia; Indianapolis and Terre Haute, Indiana; and Gainesville, Florida
- A church worker (youth division superintendent, assistant Dorcas leader, adult Sabbath School teacher, Master Guide, usher, assistant Adventist Youth Leader, and deaconess)
- A camp counselor and director of ladies at Camp Wagner in Cassopolis, Michigan, and Victory Lake Camp in Hyde Park, New York

Yes, I took a leave from everything and enrolled in Southwestern Adventist College's Adult Degree Program. That is to say that I took correspondence courses, for two and a half years. God and I sat in my daughter's dining room from 7:00 a.m. to midnight, and some nights later than that, trying to get all of my many assignments done. The only thing on my mind during this period of my life was Jesus Christ, Southwestern College, and my church duties. I had little time for anything else. The classes were heavy, but God handled the

load. There were many days and nights where I looked at all the many assignments that I had completed that day and wondered how and when I did all of them. It was then that I knew God was holding my hand and would see me through.

I was determined to get a college degree no matter what. So before I began any of my studies, I talked to God about my limitations. It had been a while since I had taken my last courses, and I knew that only God could bring back to my remembrance what I needed to know in order to achieve my goals in life. I have to say that it was not easy for me to go back to school after all of those years of being out of the academic environment, but with God all things were made possible.

I marched down the aisle of that big auditorium with 278 graduates. That was one of the most important and exciting days in my life. I then felt complete, and I knew from that experience that I really could do all things though Christ. He strengthened me.

So in 1996 after many sacrifices, sleepless nights, and answered prayers, my dream of becoming a college graduate became a reality. I received my Bachelor of Science degrees in psychology, religion, and home healthcare administration. Thanks be to God for His faithfulness to each of us.

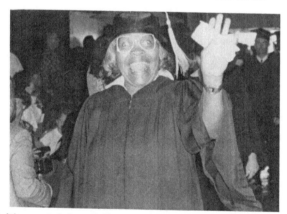

My special day. College graduation from Southwestern Seventh-day Adventist University in Keene, Texas.

Chapter 12

Florida Part 2: Home Once Again

Moving back home in 1999 was nothing but another blessing to me and my family. God renovated our family home built by the hands of my father, Tommie Lewis. Returning to live here has truly been God's special gift of memories to me.

 It is here that I now continue to give Bible studies and prison ministry training. Though I have retired from career work, I am still on the battlefield for my Lord. Visiting nursing homes, the sick and shut-in, and even making trips to the hospital, have remained part of my daily service to God. So, even though the old neighbors are all gone, God gave me new ones to tell of His love and to serve. This is all I have ever wanted to do with God's time.

My siblings (All twelve of us)

The Holy Spirit speaks to me, and I am free and in good health to go where He sends me! Praise God from whom all blessings flow! You too can thank God for His rich blessings by giving and living a life of service.

Even at this stage in my life, God has opened doors for me to begin a new ministry. While involved in a prison ministry session one day, one of the prison chaplains suggested that I should attend a meeting that trains citizens in community care. This meant that I would now be a part of the local police citizen's academy. The awesome president, Erther Wright, and my dynamic teacher,

Citizen Academy float for Homecoming. I am in the driver's seat making noise with the sireen.

James Albright, of this academy worked together to produce graduates who were dedicated to keeping our communities strong and safe.

In today's world, this is a much-needed work. This area of service totally blended all of my areas of ministry in such a way that I decided to become certified and give full service to my community. This experience has taught me even more about assisting those in need around the city's neighborhoods. Seeing up close how our police officers take chances in putting their lives in danger for the safety of strangers has really helped me to realize the seriousness of the times in which we live. This makes me want to do more and more in my small ministries and possibly make law enforcements' job a little easier.

I love what I do. My life is totally entrenched in service, and I am fulfilled in the love of Jesus Christ. It's that joy, peace, and happiness that our Lord teaches in His Word that I now have in my heart. You, too, will only know that joy, peace, and happiness (rather single or not) if you just pray and stay in God's

Graduation day from Gainesville Police Academy with Director Albright, June 8, 2004.

71

Word daily. It's all there, free of charge. Single parents—try ministry—try Jesus. He will never ever fail you! Just ask Him for ministerial direction and praise Him in advance for what He is getting ready to do in your life!

Chapter 13

Final Statement for the Single Parent

Single parents, you can achieve and reach your potential. There are no obstacles to stop you when Christ is in your life. Just as God blessed me with my college education at the age of 62, there may be personal goals or dreams that you have as well. Neither age or finances, nor any of life's difficulties can stop you.

When you step out on faith and let the Lord lead those steps, nothing but happiness will follow, and that is not to say that there will not be any trials and tribulations along the way. God's Word tells us that you are never alone (Isaiah 41:10) and that Jesus is ever present with you no matter what comes your way. Jesus is always near and there is no need to fear.

Reader, I want you to know that God will make a way out of no way when you put your total trust in Him. You must have faith, hope, and believe in God. It is only through Jesus

73

that we find the answers to today's problems, trials, crises, and all other painful situations.

Here are my final statements to the single parent.

- For the widow, Jesus is the answer. Romance Him.
- For the divorced parent, wait on the Lord to say when.
- For the young lady looking for a mate, stop looking! What's for you is for you. Jesus has already found your Mr. Right. So be faithful until that day when God sends Him to you.
- Continue to get your education. This is your time to work on "you."
- Jesus wants all of us to be happy, not lonely while here on earth.
- Being our Creator, God knows what is best for each one of us. He only commands us to obey Him daily and in order to do that we must study God's Word each day and pray without ceasing.
- God makes everything beautiful, in HIS time.
- Give a life of service to God, family, church, and community, and watch life's problems dissipate.
- Let go and let God handle all of your problems.
- Learn how to fast and pray!

I pray for all widows, divorcees, and single parents. Just remember this, if nothing else in this book helps you, JE-SUS DIED JUST FOR YOU AND HE LOVES YOU VERY MUCH. Please obey Him. Your only hope in this life is found in a relationship with God that is based on obedience to His Word. John 14:15 says, "If you love me, keep my commandments." May God bless you and yours as you turn it all over to Him. He is ABLE.

Much love to you all!

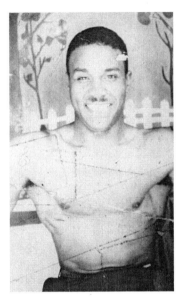

My husband, Lunue Fentress Bethea, nickname Lenny

Me, Maxine Bethea

My Children

Purette and sons: Aaron, Arion, and Arell

*Belinda and
husband, Dallas*

Debra

My Children

Son, Cochise, and wife, Joan

*My 2-year-old deceased
daughter, Vera Lunue Bethea*

*My oldest sister (deceased) and
her husband, Pastor and Mrs.
Malcolm Phipps*

77

My Grandchildren

Aaron, Arell, and Arion Mills
The Mills' Brothers' Trio

Arell

Arion, Purette (mom),
and Aaron

My Grandchildren

Skynetta Wood-Moore

Tanya Bethea

Brian Bethea

My Great-Grandchildren

Skynetta

Skyler

Skyrece

Me, Maxine Bethea

9 781572 584976